Got Quilts?

Fast and Fun Accessories From Unfinished Quilts

Pam Damour

About the Author

Known as the "Decorating Diva" Pam learned early in life, while spending time on her grandparents' farm, that making something from "scratch" was not only a way of life but it was the better way of doing things. Holding on to those values she went from farm to fabric and has had a very successful 30+ year career as an interior designer and sewing professional. Pam offers professional drapery workroom training to the trade and consumers. As a seasoned career speaker, she travels internationally teaching her specialty techniques that have brought her years of continued business as the "Couture of Home Dec Sewing". A quilter by passion, she's the author of *Pillow Talk, Cheaper By the Dozen, Got Quilts?* and producer of 12 Home Dec DVDs. Pam enjoys the hands-on aspect of the window treatment industry and has developed a 12-part template system to make custom window treatments that's taking the industry by storm! Pam lives on the shore of Lake Champlain in a log home with her husband, nestled at the foot of the Adirondack Mountains, where she teaches sewing retreats and her Window Treatment Boot Camp. Her down to earth nature, never forgetting her roots, combined with her professionalism creates a warm and creative experience. To attend one of Pam's events, go to www.pamdamour.com or to book an event for your sewing group, contact her at pam@pamdamour.com.

Introduction

Sew Sisters Publishers

PAM DAMOUR THE DECORATING DIVA
495 Point Au Fer Road
Champlain, New York 12919
pam@pamdamour.com
www.pamdamour.com
ISBN: 978-0-9848425-2-0

Photography:
Pam Damour

Cover design, book layout, and index:
Elaine Cloutier

Proofreaders:
*Penny Pombrio,
Carolyn Wells,
Betty Mitchell*
and *Sue Donohue*

Manufactured in U.S.A.

They say "It takes a village", and that's what it took to get this book finished. I started this book three years ago, just after I finished writing "Cheaper by the Dozen". When most of the projects were completed, I took them to the Sewing and Stitchery Expo in Puyallup, Washington for a trunk show promoting the new book. The day after the show, in downtown Seattle, my rental car was broken into and all my samples from this book, from *Cheaper by the Dozen* and from *Pillow Talk* were stolen. It was one of the worst days of my life. . .All my teaching samples were gone. . .A sewing educator's worst nightmare had come true. Needless to say, I had to spend the next two years recreating everything from my two books already in print, so this book was put on the back burner. The next task was to find more unfinished quilts, as I had used them up making the first round of samples. I searched yard sales, auctions, begged from my friends and yes, even bought a few on Ebay. My "Village" is my network of sewing/quilting friends and family members. Without their help and support this book would not have been possible. This book is dedicated to them and all my quilting peeps out there who have unfinished quilt projects screaming to be finished! I give you permission to cut them up, and reconstruct them into something fun and functional.

Front Row (L-R)
Carolyn Wells
Pam Damour
Betty Mitchell

Not Pictured
Diane Billerman

Back Row (L-R)
Sue Donohue
Velma Peryea
Monica Miller
Kay Kerns
Penny Pombrio
Terry Speer

A Word of Thanks

I want to thank my husband Joe for all his patience. Not very many husbands would be as gracious and entertaining with a house full of women for weeks at a time. You rock! And thank you to my mom, Marie Miller of Maw & Paw Quilt shop for coming to my rescue when I needed fabric.

I wish to thank everyone involved in making this possible.

Thank you to all these companies who believe in me and support my projects: Babylock, Bernina, Brother, Janome, Robison Anton Thread, Intressa Thread, Signature Thread, Stella Lighting, Tin Lizzie and Fairfield Processing.

Thank you to Penny Pombrio, my operations manager whose cheerful energy makes every day at work a joy!

And a special thank you to all my loyal students who follow me on Facebook, take my classes and workshops and purchase my products. You are the reason why I work so hard to develop new ideas and techniques.

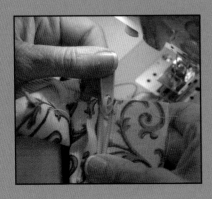

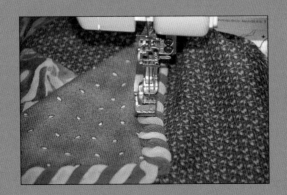

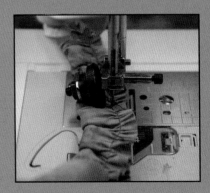

Contents

Each project has spools of difficulty ranging from 1-5.

 1 being the easiest,
5 being the most difficult.
SAMPLE - DIFFICULTY 2

 Products available at
pamdamour.com

Contents

Basic Instructions

BOX PLEAT TRIM

Now you can make perfect box pleat trim, just by lining up the numbers on our Box Pleat Tape. You can make perfect box pleats from 1" to 4" in a snap, without measuring. All pleats are true box pleats, so allow 3 times fullness the desired finish length.

Supplies
- Box Pleat Tape
- Bias fabric cut 2X the finished width, plus 1" for seam allowances by 3 times the finished length.
- Open Toe Foot
- Brass Stiletto

To Make 1" Pleats
- Place tape on your fabric about 1-2" from where you'll be sewing. Find your first "1". (It may be in a line by itself, or in a line with a "2"). Fold it down to the next "1". Find the next "1" and fold it up to the previous "1". As you make each fold, lining up the numbers, reverse the direction to create "boxes". Repeat until you have the box pleated trim you require for your project.

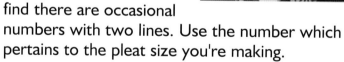

- To make 2", 3" or 4" pleats, proceed in the same manner, lining up like numbers. You will find there are occasional numbers with two lines. Use the number which pertains to the pleat size you're making.

Additional Trims
- You can also make these two trims with the box pleat tape.

Basic Instructions

CONTINUOUS PRAIRIE POINTS

Prairie points have for years been a favorite finishing technique of quilters. Having to cut, fold and pin all those little squares can be so daunting. Prairie points are made easy with the Prairie Point Ruler.

Supplies

- 1" Continuous Prairie Point Ruler
- Rotary cutter and mat
- Fabric to make into prairie points

To Make

- Lay the Prairie Point Ruler on the fabric and cut along the edges and all the slots.

- With an iron, fold and press, according to the directions on the ruler.

- After each point has been pressed twice, you can either fold them one over the other, or one inside the other.

Alternating Points

- To make points with two alternating fabrics, sew two pieces of fabric together and follow above instructions. (Part of the paper backing was removed from the ruler to better see the seam between the two fabrics.)

Basic Instructions

CONTINUOUS BIAS

Continuous bias is a term that refers to the technique where fabric is sewn into a tube, then cut in a spiral fashion to create bias strips in a very fast and efficient manner. It requires no more fabric than cutting straight grain strips of fabric.

- Begin with a square or rectangle of fabric. We're showing a rectangle, as most of the time, your fabric will be rectangular; and remember that a square is just a rectangle with 4 equal sides.

- Trim off a 45° angle of fabric as shown.

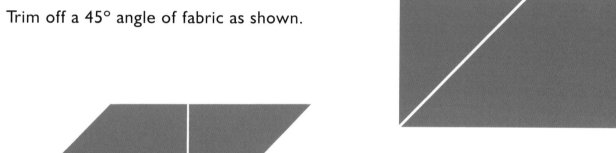

- Slide the triangle over to the other side.

- With right sides together, sew the pieces together using a 1/2" seam allowance.

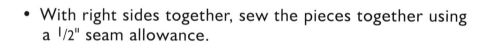

- Press seam open creating a parallelogram.

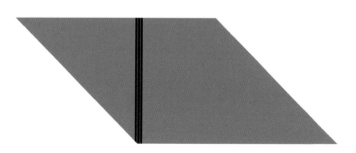

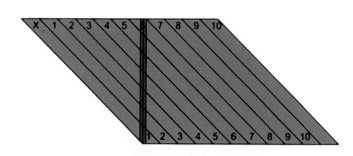

- Draw lines on the WRONG side of the fabric, the width of your desired bias strips. Number your strips as shown.

Basic Instructions

CONTINUOUS BIAS (CONTINUED)

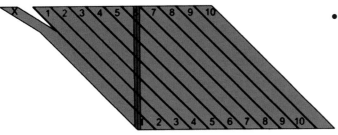

- Cut about 2" on the line between the "X" and #1.

- Line up the numbered strips so the same numbers are together. With right sides together, pin making sure like numbered strips are aligned and stitch a 1/2" seam. Press all seams open and flat. Cut on the drawn lines to create easy, uniform bias strips.

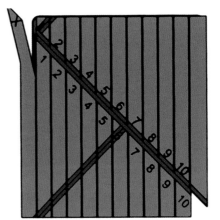

This bias can be used for single welt cord, double welt cord, ruffles, ruching, shirred welting, bias binding and banding.

MATH FORMULAS FOR CALCULATING CONTINUOUS BIAS

_____ X _____ ÷ _____ = _____ ÷ 36
Length of Bias   Width of Bias   Width of Material   Amount of Inches

= _____
   Amount in Yards

OR If you have a piece of fabric and want to know how much bias it will yield:

_____ X _____ ÷ _____ = _____ ÷ 36
Length of Fabric   Width of Fabric   Width of Bias Needed   Total Bias in Inches

= _____
   Total Bias in Yards

DOUBLE WELT CORD

Unlike single welt cord, which is inserted into a seam, double welt is an applied trim. After it's made, it can be stitched down, glued, stapled or applied with Permanent Double Stick Tape. ✏
It makes a great trim for upholstery, headboards, and pillows, just to name a few.

Supplies

* Double Welting or Double Piping Foot.

Other Requirements

* 2 1/2" wide bias the length required.
* Standard Welt Cord ✏ (or size 5/32") twice the finished length of the bias.

To Make Double Welt Cord

* Fold 1/3 of left side of bias over welt cord.

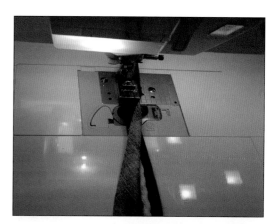

* Using polyester invisible thread in the bobbin, stitch at center needle position, with 3.0 stitch length, encasing the left side of the double welt. The wrong side will be up.

* Using another section of cord, fold over the other side of bias and stitch down the center between the two rows of cord.

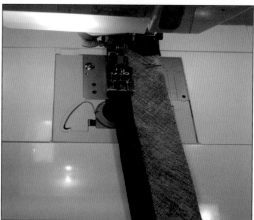

DOUBLE WELT CORD (CONTINUED)

- Trim off any excess fabric.

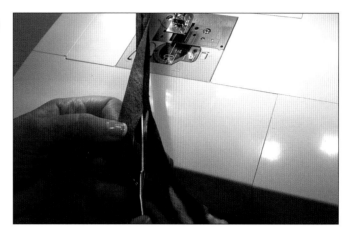

- Using hemostats, pull each cord out about $5/8$", and trim off.

- Pull fabric ends out flat and fold over end to finish, or sew flat ends into the seams of your project.

- Turn double welt over and use trimmed side down.

- Stitch down in place by sewing down the middle, or secure with staples, glue or use permanent double stick tape.

Basic Instructions

KNIFE PLEAT TRIM

Making perfect trim has never been easier. With this tape you can make knife pleats 1", 2" and 3" long. (Knife pleats are all folded in the same direction.)

Supplies

- Knife Pleat Tape
- Bias fabric cut 2X the finished width, plus 1" for seam allowances by 3 times the finished length
- Open Toe Foot
- Brass Stiletto

To Make

- To make 1" knife pleats, place tape on your fabric, with the numbers upright.

- Bring the first 2-1- line to the -1- line, stitch to secure, then bring up the second -1- to the next -1- line, stitch and repeat these two steps.

- To make 2" pleats, start with the 2-1- line and bring up to the -2- line. Repeat.

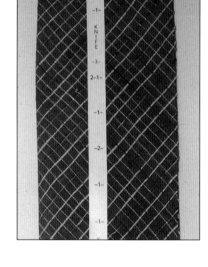

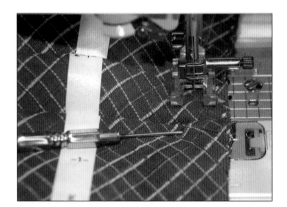

- To make 3" pleats, look for the first 6" gap between -3- lines. Bring the bottom -3- line up 6" to the next -3- line. Repeat.

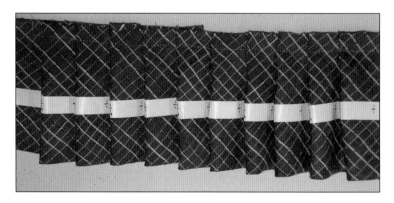

RUCHING

Ruching has always been one of my favorite finishing techniques, It is often compared to "Puffing" which is similar and used in heirloom sewing. The big difference between the two is that Ruching is made with the Ruffler Foot, and the overall length can be more accurately calculated.

Supplies

- Ruffler made specifically for your sewing machine
- Bias fabric cut 3x longer than desired finished length and 1" wider than desired finished width

Optional

- Piping foot to make corded Ruching.

To Make

- Use the Ruffler to gather your Ruching, with the setting on "1". Gather both sides of fabric.

Note: *It's recommended to gather a sample to gauge your fullness. Put two marks 12" apart and test until they are 4" apart, for a three times fullness. Adjust the ruffler by tightening or loosening the set screw, and/or adjusting the stitch length.*

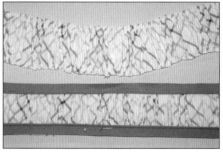

- If one side of your Ruching is longer, (which it often is) sew welt cord to the smaller side first. Then, pin cord onto the other side, arranging gathers to keep them even.

Shirred Welting

- The beauty of Ruching is that if you fold it over, and sew the edges over a fat cord, you have perfect shirred welting.

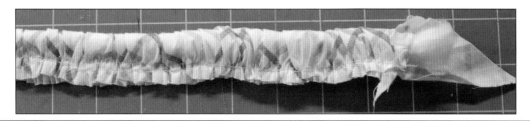

Basic Instructions

THE ULTIMATE PILLOW TEMPLATE ✎

The hardest part of making pillows is knowing where to mark for cutting. We always use a pillow template when marking the cutting line for pillows. This provides accurate sizes, as well as the ability to center the pattern, and get a visual of how the finished project is going to look.

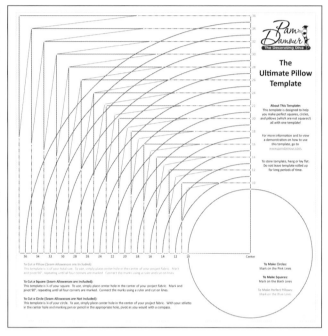

The Ultimate Pillow Template was designed to mark for squares, circles and pillows. Use a chalk liner or Frixion Pen when making your lines so marks can be removed if needed. To use, center the corner circle over your fabric and mark one fourth of shape using holes in the template. Rotate template 90°, and mark in the holes. Repeat this two more times.

- The blue lines are for pillows and include seam allowances.

- The black lines are for squares and do not include seam allowances.

- The pink lines are for circles. This template can be used to make pillows, squares and circles from 10" to 36". For a video clip on how to use this, go to www.pamdamour.com.

- If doing a placket zipper insertion, cut the bottom edge of your pillow straight first, cut your placket after cutting both pillow top and bottom. Match grain lines when cutting placket. Refer to Basic Instructions for Zipper Insertion, page 20.

- Use the blue lines to trim the "Dog Ears".

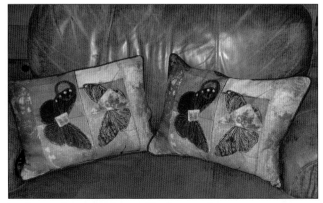

"Dog Ears" are cute on Chrissie but not on pillows!

Left with template, Right without template

Note: *For template information, refer to the Products List on page 72.*

WELT CORD

Welt Cord (or piping cord) comes in many sizes. The standard in home decorating is about $1/4"$ across, micro welt is about $1/8"$ across, and jumbo welt is about $1/2"$ across. Welt cord is the perfect trim when you want a little something extra and it doesn't require very much fabric.

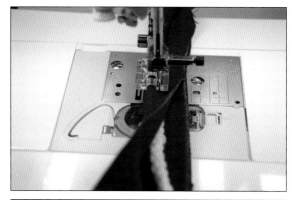

Supplies

- Depending on which foot you have, use either the $1/4"$ Welt Cord Foot, the Piping Foot or a Zipper Foot.

- $1-1/2"$ to 2" or $2-1/4"$ wide bias, depending on which size welting you're making.

- Welt Cord to be covered

- Brass Stiletto

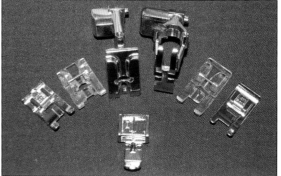

To Make

Fold bias strip over welt cord, and place under presser foot with the cord under the deep groove of the welt cord foot. With a left groove in your foot, center needle position with a stitch length of 3.0, move needle 2 positions to the right. If your foot has a center groove, move your needle all the way to the right.

- Or if you don't own a machine with a $1/4"$ Welt Cord Foot, use your Zipper Foot, and move the needle all the way over to the left, lining up with the edge of the foot.

- Trim after sewing using the Pam Damour Home Dec Ruler to get an accurate $1/2"$ seam allowance.

To Sew Welt onto Fabric

- Using welt cord already made, move one needle position to the right. Place raw edges of welt cord with edge of fabric. Sew welt cord onto fabric, stitching between the original stitching line and the cord.

Corners

- To turn the corner, make three snips, all the way to the stitching line. The center snip should be at $1/2"$ from the edge of the project.

WELT CORD (CONTINUED)

- Turn the corner, and using your stiletto, push the fabric back into the corner. Sew into place. Repeat this for the remaining three corners.

Splicing the Cord

- To join the cord, sew all the way around leaving about a 2" space from where the cord started.

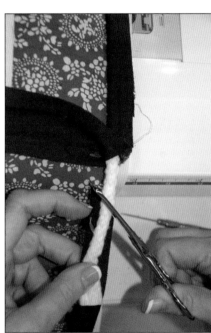

- Trim the beginning end at a 45 degree angle.

- Trim the ending section straight across, with about a 2" overlap.

- Rip the stitching out of the ending section, and trim the welt cord at the same 45 degree angle as the beginning end.

- Fold the unstitched fabric over, wrong sides together at a 45 degree angle as shown.

- Fold over and sew in place, holding everything together with a stiletto.

WELT CORD (CONTINUED)

Micro Welt

- When making Micro Welt use a foot with a smaller groove or a zipper foot. Trim to a $1/2$" seam allowance using the Home Dec Ruler.

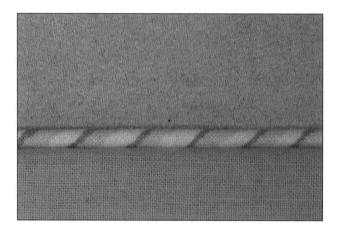

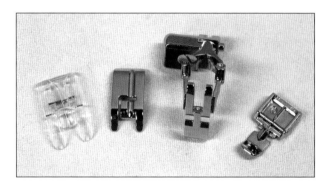

Jumbo Welt

- When making a Jumbo Welt, you can use a zipper foot with the needle moved all the way to the left.

Note: *I found that engaging the built in dual feeder helped to keep the bias from shifting.*

- Another helpful foot used in make jumbo welt is the leather wheel pictured here with other feet used.

ZIPPER INSERTIONS

Supplies
- Zipper Foot or Double Welting Foot
- Zipper Tape

Placket Insertion
- For pillows, cut front and back the same size, plus cut an additional 2" wide strip of fabric the width of the pillow back, using the same grain line as the bottom edge of the pillow. This 2" piece will be used for the zipper placket.

- Press under a $1/2$" seam allowance on the top edge of the pillow back. You can serge the edges prior to pressing under if you'd like a cleaner finish inside.

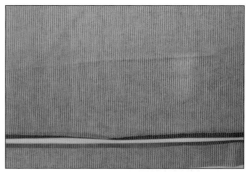

- Cut the Zipper Tape to the needed length and sew the folded placket edge close to the zipper teeth.

- The Zipper Foot should be attached on the left side hanging off the right side with the needle position all the way to the left. If using a double welting foot, use the left groove.

- After stitching the zipper to the placket, reattach the Zipper Foot to the other side, and move the needle to the far right position. If using a Double Welt Foot, zipper teeth should be in the right groove. Place the pillow back fabric over the zipper to create a flap, keeping the zipper foot next to the zipper; topstitch the back in place.

Basic Instructions

ZIPPER INSERTIONS (CONTINUED)

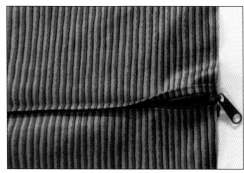

- Separate the zipper several inches and insert the slide. Leave the slide near the center of the pillow.

- With right sides together, lay the pillow front on top of the pillow back. Trim the back to match the size of the pillow front, leaving about $1/2$" to $3/4$" of placket remaining to be sewn into the seam. The goal is to make the zipper appear as if it is along the bottom edge of the pillow.

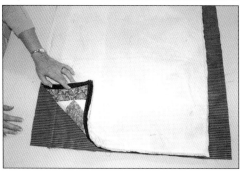

Note: The exception is when your making a flange as shown here. Be sure to have the zipper above the flange stitching line.

- Sew the pillow back and front together, using a single welt foot for easier sewing and a more consistent seam allowance. Trim the corners and clean-finish the seams. Open the zipper and turn the pillow right side out.

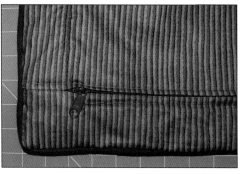

Rise Insertion

- When making a box-style cushion, the height of the cushion is referred to as the "rise". Sewing a cushion with a rise requires a different zipper insertion, as the cushion cover requires a larger opening for the cushion insert. Generally, the zipper on a box-style cushion requires some extra length to travel a few inches around a corner as well as the entire back edge. Be sure to allow about 8" of extra fabric all the way around for ease in the rise.

- Cut the rise 1" deeper than the thickness of the desired cushion height. For the zipper placket, cut two rises each the depth of the front rise plus $1/4$". For standard rectangular cushion, the zipper portion of the rise should be the entire back of the cushion, plus travel around two corners. Allow 4" to 6" for each end of the zipper in addition to the back width of the cushion.

- Fold the zipper placket in half, lengthwise, with wrong sides together. Sew with the folded edge close to the zipper teeth. The Zipper Foot should be attached on the right side with the needle position all the way to the left.

ZIPPER INSERTIONS (CONTINUED)

- After stitching the zipper down, re-attach the zipper foot to the other side of the ankle and bring the needle to the far right position. Overlap the fabric slightly to create a flap and topstitch in place.

- Separate the zipper a couple inches and insert the slide. Place the slide in the center of the zipper to continue.

- Sew the zipper placket onto pillow front first, leaving 2-3" unsewn at each end to attach to rise front.

- Starting at the center front of the cushion, sew the rise to the cushion top all the way to the corner. Snip the rise 1/2" at the corner and turn the corner. Leave 2" unsewn at each end to join the zipper placket.

- Where the two rise sections join, trim off any excess of the two inches allowed and sew across the ends.

- Sew the tucks down flat.

Note: *The purpose of the flaps is they act as a "fudge factor" so you can adjust if necessary. It also protects and takes the stress off the ends of the zipper when adding fill or a form.*

Bottom Edge Insertion

- The Bottom Edge Insertion is used when there's no trim to get in the way of a zipper, or when there are two or more trims, and it's easier to hide a zipper in the bottom seam between trims. It's a cleaner application, but with trims involved, it can be a bit trickier. It's also the best technique to use for a totally concealed zipper, as invisible zippers aren't used in the decorating industry.

- When making a bottom edge insertion, cut the desired length of zipper tape, allowing for seam allowances.

Basic Instructions

ZIPPER INSERTIONS (CONTINUED)

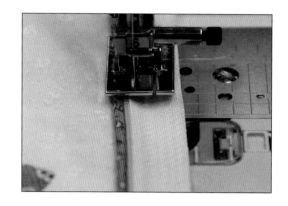

- Separate zipper and sew one side hugged up to the welt cord, with right sides together, using a double welting foot.

- Sew the back side of the pillow using the other side of the zipper foot, sewing both sides of the zipper in the same direction to prevent any torquing.

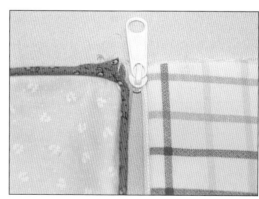

- With the zipper tab up, insert both ends of the zipper teeth into the rounded end of the slide.

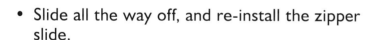

- Slide all the way off, and re-install the zipper slide.

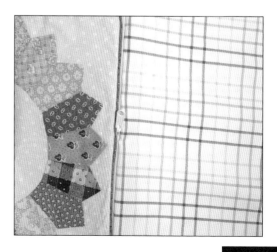

- Stop slide in the center, leaving both ends of the zipper tape sealed.

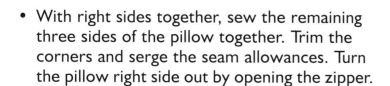

- With right sides together, sew the remaining three sides of the pillow together. Trim the corners and serge the seam allowances. Turn the pillow right side out by opening the zipper.

Basic Instructions

RIC RAC TRIM

Ric Rac trim is easy and fun to make. I love it because I always have lots of Ric Rac trim in my stash. I believe this technique has been around for a while, but I hadn't seen it until my friend, Sue Donohue showed me how to make it when I was prepping for a webinar.

Supplies
- 2 pieces of same size Ric Rac
- A pin-able surface to hold your work
- A sturdy T-pin or straight pin
- Steam Iron

To Make
- Begin by anchoring both pieces of Ric Rac together with the T-pin.

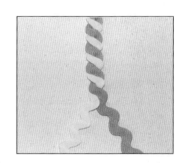

- Start by wrapping one side over the other. (I'm left handed so wrap with left over right. If you're right handed, right over left may feel more natural to you.)

- Continue to wrap, always with the same side on top.

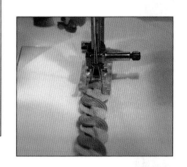

- Press frequently with a good steam iron.

- Sew down the middle, either using a decorative stitch, a zig zag or use a 4-6mm twin needle. You can also use your serger chain stitch or cover stitch.

- This trim can be sewn right onto your project or it can be used as a strap for a bag.

QUILT TOP HEADBOARD

Covering your headboard can be one of the trickiest projects in this book, but at the same time can be the most rewarding. A custom upholstered headboard from a decorator can start well over $1,000, and the bigger the headboard, the bigger the price. A pieced covering to your headboard can add homey comfort to your bedroom without breaking the bank. The key is to use what you already have. When I first started writing this book, I used an antique wooden headboard that I picked up in my neighborhood from my neighbor's bulk trash pile. (Yes, I have no pride). My first thought was, "Hey, I can do something fun with this!" (See before & after shots!!) Then

something horrible happened. . .My rental car was broken into and all my samples for this book were stolen. I've spent the last two years recreating all my samples, and since I didn't have the original quilts any more, many of my color palettes were changed. Originally I used two quilt tops to make the headboard cover, bedskirt, shams and bolster for a full size bed. At the end of this chapter, I'm including the original instructions for using the wooden headboard. This cover has a ruched edge with Micro Welt Cord on each edge of the Rushing.

Supplies

- Headboard to be covered
- Quilt top
- Cotton drapery lining
- Fabric for Ruching
- Fabric for headboard back
- Batting

- Fantastic Fusible Fabric Backing®
- Basting spray (optional)
- Ruffler
- Piping Foot
- Hook & Loop Tape for the bottom edge
- Micro Welt Cord

In writing this book, I found this quilt top, which at 96" square, was large enough to cut a bedskirt, headboard and sham. Here is the before shot of the quilt top, and the lay out used to cut out the projects in this book.

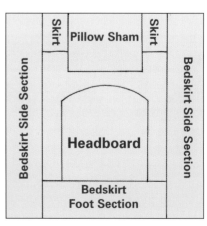

QUILT TOP HEADBOARD (CONTINUED)

To Make

- Measure the headboard to be covered. If it needs any padding, measure after padding for a good fit.

- Use drapery lining or white cotton to make a pattern. This piece will be used to line the quilt top front.

- Before cutting the quilt top apart, fuse with Fantastic Fusible Fabric Backing 🪡 to keep seams from coming apart.

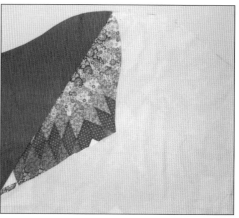

- Use the drapery lining pattern to cut front and back. The back is cut from a coordinating fabric.

- Pin lining to quilt top to keep from shifting or use a temporary quilter's basting spray.

Ruching

- To make a Ruched edge, please refer to the Basic Instructions, page 15.

- Sew Micro Welt Cord onto each edge of Ruching. Please refer to Basic Instructions, page 19.

- Pin finished Ruching onto headboard front and sew using 1/2" seam allowances.

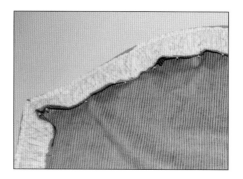

- Starting in the center of the headboard and working out, pin ruching to headboard back, to match front.

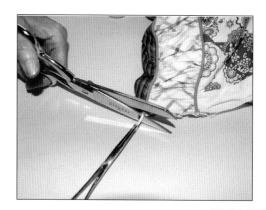

- Pull out about 3/4" of cord at each end of the ruching. By doing this, the fabric will fold easier when making a rolled hem at the bottom.

QUILT TOP HEADBOARD (CONTINUED)

- Serge all the seams, or secure with a zig zag stitch.

- Place the cover over headboard, and trim bottom to fit. Secure with Hook & Loop Tape. This head board is mounted with a Headboard Mounting Cleat ✐ which will be installed directly on the wall.

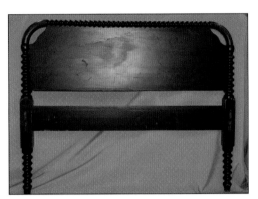

- If covering an existing headboard, similar to this one, you will have to add padding to cover the wood details.

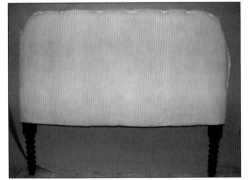

- Here is the headboard with padding.

To Finish a Headboard with Legs:

- After both sides are sewn, roll bottom edge of Ruching. To determine the fit, put the cover on the headboard and mark your stitching line.

- Depending on the size of your headboard leg, this will be custom fit.

QUILT TOP HEADBOARD (CONTINUED)

- Mark for cutting away for the leg of the headboard.

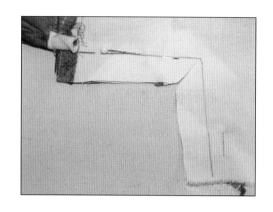

- Allow for 1/2" seam allowance and cut out.

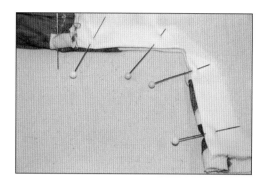

- Fold edges to the inside, and pin into place.

- Top stitch closed.

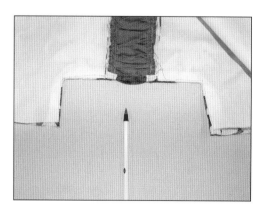

- Serge or zig-zag seam allowances and bottom edges.

- Add Hook & Loop Tape to the bottom flaps.

Patchwork Bedskirt

PATCHWORK BEDSKIRT

Using our Lone Star quilt top, the border was cut off to create a tailored bedskirt. As with all my custom bedskirts, this one is lined with white drapery lining.

Supplies

- Quilt top: King or Queen
- Drapery Lining:
  Twin/Full: 5 yards of 54" wide home dec lining
  Queen/King: 7 $1/2$ yards of 54" home dec lining
- $3/4$ yards coordinating fabric (optional) for deck banding
- Katie Lane Scallop Radial Rule (optional)

Before beginning your bedskirt, you must first measure your bed to achieve the correct size. In the past few years mattresses have become thicker and box springs sizes have varied too. Measure the box spring from the top edge to the floor. If you have hardwood floors, deduct $1/2$" from this measurement. If you have carpeting, deduct 1". This will be your finished length or drop.

Bed Sizes

Twin size bed 39" by 75"
Full size bed 54" by 75"
Queen size bed 60" by 80"
King size bed 78" by 80"

Bedskirt

- Your bedskirt will consist of three rectangles: two larger ones for the sides, and one small for the foot. Use the following formula:

- From the long sides of the quilt, cut 2 strips (the finished length plus 1 $1/2$") by 108" for twin/full and 113" for queen/king. If quilt top isn't long enough, you may need to add additional fabric on each end.

- From the short sides of the quilt top, cut two strips (the finished length plus 1 $1/2$") that will add up to the width of the bed plus 20".

Patchwork Bedskirt

PATCHWORK BEDSKIRT (CONTINUED)

Bedskirt Lining

- The following cuts should be made from the finished length of bedskirt. From 54" wide lining, cut the following 2" shorter than the bedskirt cuts:
  Twin bed: 6 cuts
  Full bed: 6 cuts
  Queen bed: 6 cuts
  King bed: 7 cuts

- Seam lining cuts together with serger and press seams. They will be cut into pieces later.

- Once you make the cuts as shown on the diagram, add necessary pieces to make the size you need.

- After each of the three bedskirt sections are cut, sew lining along the bottom edge only. Press seam allowances toward the lining.

- To sew the skirt sides, line the top edge of the lining to the top edge of the skirt. Because the skirt is 2" longer than the lining, this will cause the skirt fabric to wrap around to the back, and make a facing.

- After each of the skirt sections is sewn on the sides, turn right sides out and press.

- The skirt sides will be pleated like this: One 4" pleat at the head of the bed, one 4" pleat at the foot of the bed with a 1" overlap at each corner and a center double pleat with a 4" deep pleat on the center of each side. This should measure about 74" for a twin/full and 79" for queen/king. You may need to adjust if it doesn't.

Bedskirt Decking

- Twin: cut one width of 54" fabric, by 76" long
- Full: cut one width of 54" fabric, by 76" long
- Queen: cut two widths of 54" fabric, by 81" long, and sew together
- King: cut two widths of 54" fabric, by 81" long, and sew together.

PATCHWORK BEDSKIRT (CONTINUED)

Prepare the Deck

- Trim bedskirt deck to fit box spring top.

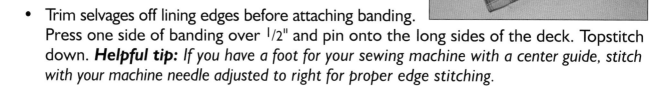

- Use the remaining quilt fabric or a coordinating fabric and cut enough banding 5" wide to surround the three sides of the bedskirt.

- Trim selvages off lining edges before attaching banding. Press one side of banding over ¹/2" and pin onto the long sides of the deck. Topstitch down. ***Helpful tip:*** *If you have a foot for your sewing machine with a center guide, stitch with your machine needle adjusted to right for proper edge stitching.*

- Stitch the remaining banding to the bottom or foot end of the bedskirt.

Trim the Corners

- You can either make a pattern for the corner of your box spring by tracing onto card stock or you can use the Katie Lane Scallop Radial Rule ✎ template and trace the curve that best fits your bed. Mark the center of the curved corner with either a pin or notch.

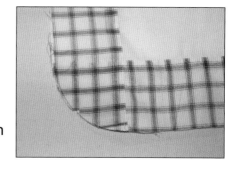

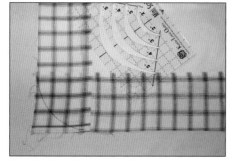

- After the skirt sections and deck sections are prepared, it's time to put them all together. Find the center of each side of the deck and each side of the bedskirt. Start with one side and pin the center of the bedskirt to the center of the deck. Bring one end to corner, overlap 1". Divide bedskirt excess in half.

- Half of the excess will be the center pleat and half will be the corner pleat. Pin other half of the bedskirt starting 1" down from the top.

- Divide this excess in half. Half will be the remainder of the center pleat with the remaining half the top pleat.

Patchwork Bedskirt

PATCHWORK BEDSKIRT (CONTINUED)

- Repeat above with other side. To complete the bottom side pin center. Work out the excess into pleats in each end.

- Pin each skirt section onto the deck, starting at the top edge, leaving 1" of deck extending to roll over and stitch down later.

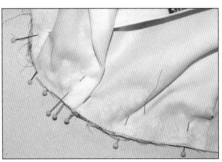

- When you get to the curved corner, the fold of the pleat should end at the center of the curve.

- The 1" overlap will tuck over the fold of the adjoining skirt section. There's often minor adjustments that need to be done to the skirt sections, so they fit correctly. Don't panic, and think you did something wrong. Fabrics can often stretch or shrink when being sewn and pressed.

- Take a deep breath; this is home dec so you'll be fine!

- After all sections are sewn with a $^1/_2$" seam allowance, finish the seams by serging or using a zig-zag stitch.

- Roll the top edge of the deck a double $^1/_2$" and topstitch.

- The easiest way to put the bedskirt on is to flip the mattress up at the head of the bed. Place the bedskirt in place, folding over at the top. After the mattress is back in place, you'll be able to slide the top part in place.

Pillow Sham

PILLOW SHAM

The Pillow Sham is a decorative pillow cover for a pillow that usually sits in front of your bed pillow. I'm often asked why my shams have a zipper in the back, rather than an overlap. The answer is simple: the flap is homemade! It's industry standard to use a zipper.

Note: *To use the layout from our quilts use the diagram to the right.*

Supplies

- Quilt top
- Lining for quilt top
- Coordinating fabric
- 10 1/4 yards of standard welt cord
- Fusi-boo fusible quilt batting
- Zipper Tape with Slides
- Zipper Foot
- Welt Foot
- Double Welt Foot
- Ultimate Pillow Template

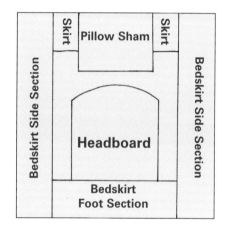

Sham Size Recommendations

Twin Bed: Use one queen: 20" by 30" or one king pillow: 20" by 36"
Full Bed: Use 2 standard pillows: 20" by 26"
Queen Bed: Use 2 queen pillows: 20" by 30"
King Bed: Use 2 king pillows: 20" by 36"

To Make

- Add 1" inch to the sham size you are making for seam allowance. Mark the cutting lines for your sham using the Ultimate Pillow Template. If possible, center your project on a particular block. This sham was cut from this section of the quilt, because it allowed for the placement of the headboard and the bedskirt. If you want to make two shams, try to make them match, if you have enough quilt top to work with. To center your motif or block, use the centering guide on the Ultimate Pillow Template. Please refer to Basic Instructions, page 16.

Pillow Sham

To Make (CONTINUED)

- To make a sham with a flange, like the one shown, add for the width of the flange. For example for a 2" sham, add 4" to the width and 4" to the height.

  Note: *This pillow sham, on a twin bed was cut 35" wide by 25" tall to accommodate a queen pillow with a 2" flange.*

- To prevent the quilt top from coming apart, fuse the quilt top, batting and lining all together using a product called "Fusi-boo" by Fairfield Processing. It's a double sided fusible batting and perfect for free motion work and washes out after it's quilted!

Sham Front

- After cutting sham front, cut a lining to match. To stabilize the patchwork, use a layer of Fusi-boo from Fairfield.

- After fusing the sham front to the batting and lining, add the welt cord. See Basic Instructions, page 17 for making and applying welt cord.

Sham Back

- Since it's more than likely that you may not have enough pieced fabric to cover both the sham front and back, choose a coordinating fabric for the back and/or welt cord trim.

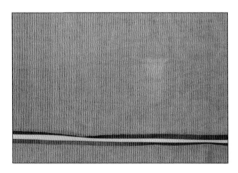

- Cut the sham back the same size as the front.

- Cut the flange 3 1/2" wide by the width of the pillow insert.

- Press the bottom of the edge under 1/2" and the top edge of the flange 1/2". This will be where your zipper goes. See Basic Instructions, page 20 for zipper (placket) insertion.

Pillow Sham

Putting Your Sham Together

- Your sham is now ready to sandwich together.

- Line up bottom edges and trim excess off the top.

Note: *You need to leave the full amount of the placket, because of the flange. If you're making a sham without a flange, cut sham front & back the same size and insert zipper into the bottom edge. See Basic Instructions, page 20 for zipper bottom insertion.*

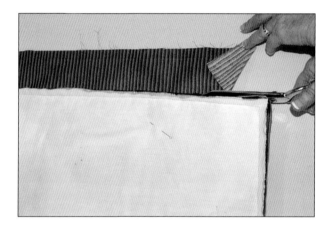

- Pin sham front to sham back, and sew together using the welt cord seam allowances as your guide. Trim corners and turn right side out. Press flat.

- To sew flange, set the quilting bar on your machine to the width of your flange. Most sewing machines have quilting bars that will extend to 3". If you don't have a quilting bar, place a section of painters tape on the bed of your machine to mark the edge of your project.

- Be sure that when sewing along the zipper placket, the zipper is to the inside edge of the sham. Reinforce the zipper by backstitching as you sew over the placket.

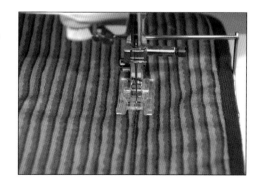

OCTAGON CUSHION

This cushion was made from the scraps of our book cover Lone Star Quilt. In order to make it large enough, we added some muslin diamond shaped pieces, and Velma spent the better part of a day putting it all back together. The octagon shape came out of what we had leftover from the quilt.

Note: The objective of this chapter is to show how to make a box style cushion, whether it's a cushion for a chair, bench, window seat or if you just want an accent cushion like this one. The shape is yours to decide! The difference between a cushion (in this country) is the rise or boxing. In other countries, such as Australia, England and New Zealand, "Pillows" are the bed pillows, "Cushions" are what we call accent pillows.

Supplies
- Quilt blocks for cushion top and/or bottom
- Fabric for cushion rise and/or cushion bottom
- Fabric to cover welt cord (a fat quarter or scraps)
- Standard Welt Cord to wrap the cushion perimeter twice, plus an additional 10" for splicing
- Pam's Perfect Puff & Stuff® polyester stuffing
- 18" Zipper Tape & one slide
- Fantastic Fusible Fabric Backing
- 2-1" decorative or covered buttons
- Heavy duty thread and long hand sewing needle

To Make
- Use leftover quilt blocks or cut this from an existing quilt top. Our cushion measures 18" across, so it was cut 19" across.

- Add a fusible fabric backing to the cushion front to prevent seams from coming apart.

- Cut a lining to match and use it to line cushion front.

- Cut a corresponding cushion back from a coordinating fabric, or more pieced fabric if you have it.

FEATHERED STAR TABLECLOTH

This feathered star quilt top was a piece that I really didn't want to cut up. I thought it would make a great tablecloth because it was an octagon shape, but these directions can be used for a square or rectangular tablecloth. This tablecloth is lined, has a micro welt cord edge and is complimented with a 3 1/2" deep doubled folded knife pleat ruffle.

Supplies

- Quilt top
- Coordinating fabric for pleated ruffle and Micro Welt
- Lining fabric
- Flannel interlining
- Knife Pleat Tape
- Micro Welt Cord or beaded weight chain
- Piping Foot
- Permanent Double Stick Tape or Steam-a-Seam (optional)
- Basting Spray

To Make

- Cut lining and flannel interlining to fit quilt top. Layer the interlining on the back of the quilt top and pin together, or use basting spray.

- Cut bias 1 3/4" wide for Micro Welt. You will need enough for the perimeter of the tablecloth, plus about 3" extra for overlap.

- Using a piping foot, make Micro Welt and sew onto tablecloth. See Basic Instructions for making Continuous Bias, page 10 and Micro Welt, page 19.

Note: Adding a beaded weight chain in place of micro welt will weight down the edge and allow the table cloth to hang better.

- To make a pleated ruffle, cut ruffle twice the finished width plus an inch for seam allowances. (This one was cut 8" wide for a 3-1/2" wide ruffle).

FEATHERED STAR TABLECLOTH

(CONTINUED)

- Fold the ruffle bias in half lengthwise, with wrong sides together and press flat. See Basic Instructions, page 14, to make the Knife Pleated Ruffle.

- Pin ruffle to tablecloth front.

- Sew the pleated ruffle over the welt cord, using the same 1/2" seam allowance.

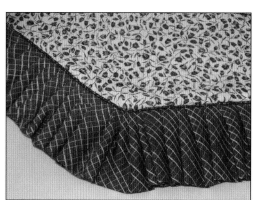

- Add extra fullness at the corners.

- Splice the ruffle by tucking one end inside the other.

- Next, sew lining onto the tablecloth front. Use the stitching line for the cord and ruffle as your guide. Clip corners.

- Leave an opening along one straight side large enough to turn right side out. Press flat.

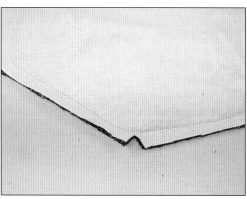

- Close opening by using either Permanent Double Stick Tape or Steam-a-Seam.

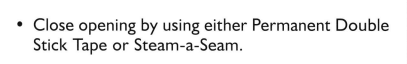

QUILT TOP ROMAN SHADE

When making a Roman Shade there are several ways of making them. I suggest that when using a quilt top; add a layer of lining or interlining to help protect the quilt top from fading.

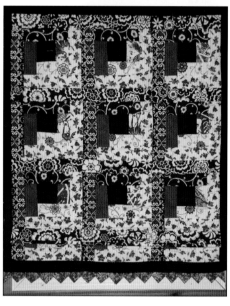

Supplies

- Quilt top or face fabric (see below for size and/or yardage)
- Lining (see below for size and/or yardage)
- Cord Lock
- Weight Bar
- Cord Tassel
- Rings (Quantities will depend on the size of shade)
- Lift cord (Quantities will depend on the size of shade)
- Screw eyes (Quantities will depend on the size of shade)
- Ribs (optional)
- Quick Points 2.0 Prairie Point Ruler (optional)
- Workroom Push Pins
- Lift Cord Adjusters
- Permanent Double Stick Tape
- Gimp Braid (enough to cover the top edge of the shade)
- Wooden Tassel

To Make

Measure your window. You need to determine where you want to mount your shade. You have two options:

- **Inside Mount:** Wood mounting board and shade are inside the window frame.
- **Outside Mount:** Wood mounting board and shade are outside the window frame. It's recommended that when doing an outside mount, add 4" to the shade length and 1" to the shade width.

Face Fabric

Measure window to be covered with shade. Add the following dimensions:

shade width	+ 2"	= cut width
shade length	+ 10"	= cut length

Optional Interlining

Measure window to be covered with shade. Add the following dimensions:

shade width	+ 2"	= cut width
shade length	+ 10"	= cut length

Lining

Add the following dimensions:

shade width	+ 0"	= cut width
shade length	+ 6"	= cut length

QUILT TOP ROMAN SHADE (CONTINUED)

CUTTING

Quilt Top or Face Fabric

Cut your fabric using the previous chart. If the quilt top you wish to use is too short or too narrow, add coordinating fabric to achieve desired size. If it's too large, carefully choose how to cut to size. You may want to center a block or motif.

This is also your opportunity to add a creative trim, such as the trim shown, made from the Quick Points 2.0 Prairie Point Ruler.

Interlining

Cut interlining the same size as the face fabric. Suggested fabric choices are:
- Drapery lining (for sun protection)
- Blackout lining (for light control and sun protection)
- Drapery interlining (for insulation and sun protection)
  Layer interlining on the wrong side of quilt top and treat as one fabric. To stabilize layers and prevent shifting, spray with a basting spray.

Lining

- Cut lining using the previous chart for lining. Press all fabrics before sewing together.

Assembly

- With the interlining pinned or spray basted to the quilt top, pin to lining with right sides together, lining up at the top.

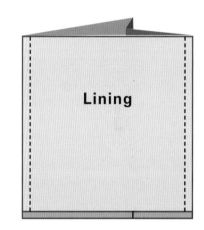

- Align the sides and sew both sides with a $1/2$" seam allowance.

- There will be an excess of face fabric, because it's cut 2" wider. (When the shade is turned right sides out, the face fabric will roll around to the back creating a $1/2$" facing.)

- Press seam allowance toward the quilt fabric. Turn right sides out and press flat. The seam allowances should be in the outer edges of the shade. If making a traditional shade hem, fold up bottom 5", and under 1", creating a 4" hem with a 1" under turn.

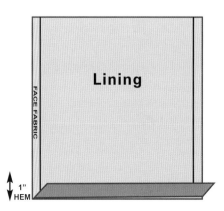

- Top stitch hem in place. Now you're ready to mark for your rings.

QUILT TOP ROMAN SHADE (CONTINUED)

Optional Prairie Points

- If you wish to add Prairie Points to the bottom, as we did here, cut 6" off the hem, add continuous Prairie Points, (See Basic Instructions, page 9) then sew hem back on. Make a 4" hem turning excess under.

Attach the Rings

- Rows of rings on the back of the shade guide the draw cords up the shade to screw eyes in the mounting board. Use 3/8" brass rings on the bottom row as they will endure the most stress. They may be attached by hand sewing, or a zigzag stitch with your sewing machine. Mark the locations for the rings beginning at the bottom quilting line at the top of the hem 1/2" from each side.

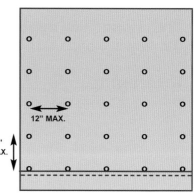

- Space the remaining rings in rows 8" to 12" apart across the width of the shade, and a height of no more than 6".

Sewing Method

- Pin through all layers at each ring location to prevent shifting while you attach the rings. Lower the machine feed dogs and sew a ring in place at each mark using a zigzag stitch through all fabric layers.

No-Sew Method

- If you wish to put the rings in quickly, use a specific T-gun which installs the rings. When using the ring gun it's recommended that the bottom row of rings be brass and sewn.

Ribs & Weight Bar

- Professionally manufactured shades have a bottom weight bar to keep the shade hanging evenly and ribs at each row of rings. Place each rib above each row of rings between the face fabric and the lining.

- After all the rings are in, snake the ribs down the shade in between the layers and let them rest above each row of rings. Cut each rib 1/4" shorter than the finished width of the shade and cut the weight bar 1/2" shorter. Set aside and prepare your mounting board.

QUILT TOP ROMAN SHADE (CONTINUED)

The Mounting Board

Using basic pine lumber cut a 1" x 2" or 1" x 3" board the width of your shade, less 1/4".

- Cover the board with leftover lining. You will want to cover it like wrapping a present using a staple gun.

- Drill mounting screw holes slightly larger than the diameter of the 2" long mounting screws. This will keep the board from splitting. Try to position them so they are not directly above the rows of rings where a screw eye will be located.

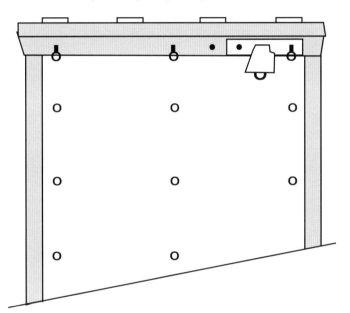

- Attach a pulley or cord lock at the side of the shade where you want to pull the cords to raise it, positioning it above the outer row of rings. Use a screw to attach the inner end of the pulley and a screw eye to attach the outer end, lining up the screw eye with the outer row of rings.

- Insert screw eyes above each of the other rows of rings, using a screw eye driver. For easier operation of very large shades, pulleys may be used in lieu of screw eyes.

- Using a square, draw a mounting line on your shade (use a marking tool which is temporary). Using large Workroom Push Pins, pin shade to the board. Measure before stapling to assure shade is straight and the right length. Staple in place, and trim away excess.

- With Permanent Double Stick Tape, glue a piece of gimp braid to cover raw edges on the mounting board.

QUILT TOP ROMAN SHADE (CONTINUED)

Stringing the Shade

- Begin stringing the cords at the row of rings below the cord lock. Feed the cord through the bottom ring and continue up through each until threading through the screw eye adjacent to the cord lock. Then thread it down through the pulley on the outward side of the cord lock wheel leaving 2 to 3 feet of cord for the draw cord. Cut it below the bottom ring, add a Lift Cord Adjuster and tie knot at the end.

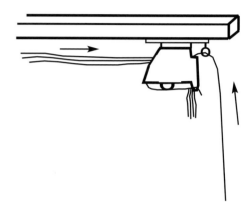

- String another cord up through the next row of rings, through the appropriate screw eye, then over and down through the pulley. Match the length of the other cord below the pulley. Cut below the bottom ring, add a cord lock adjuster and tie knot at the end.

- Repeat the process for all remaining cords.

- Tie the cords together with an overhand knot an inch below the cord lock after pulling slightly to achieve even tension on all cords. Cut all to the same length leaving them long enough so you can easily reach them when the shade is completely lowered.

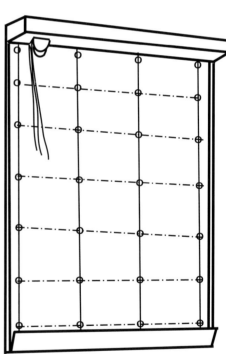

- Braid the cord ends together, and finish with a wooden tassel at the end. A large knot at the cord ends will keep the tassel from coming off.

- Now your shade is ready to install. When installing an inside mount, screw mounting board into the inside of the window frame. If installing outside the window, mount at least 4" above the trim, to give the hardware freedom to work properly.

- If the shade is hanging uneven, use the cord adjusters to level shade. Draw shade up and steam to "train" folds.

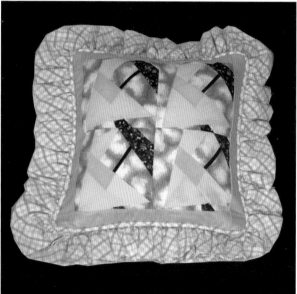

Red, Black & White Bed

From my book, *The Tangled Home*, this headboard and matching sham are made from a
quilt top to coordinate with the zentangled quilt.

Valance

Using Template Number 7 from my *Cheaper by the Dozen* Book, I made this valance from a quilt top.

Ruffled Pillow

This pillow uses four orphaned blocks of Rain Bonnet Sue, accompanied by a matching window pane plaid.

Grommet Drapery Panels

GROMMET DRAPERY PANELS

Making drapery panels from a quilt top can be a great way to use up a good-sized quilt top. The average length needed for a floor length drapery is about 100", so depending on the length of your quilt top, you may need to add more length, or make a shorter panel. There are many ways to pleat the top of your drapery panel. I've chosen my "grommet style" for its soft and casual nature which blends with the quilt top.

Supplies

- Quilt top for drapery panels
- Lining for panels
- Grommet tape with ring faces
- Drapery weights (2 for each panel)
- Edge Joining Foot
- Wrinkle Release Dressing Spray

When making standard draw draperies, here are a few hints:

Fullness: Industry standards are a minimum of 2 ¹/₂ x full, but when using a quilt top, you may have less. The minimum I'd recommend is 2 times full.

Headers: If using a 4" Buckram, allow 8" for a full cuff, for pinch pleats. For the grommet drapery, you can allow less; about 1" will be enough.

Hems: The standard is a 4" double fold (8" total); lining hems are 2" double fold (4" total).

Calculating yardage

A) <u>DETERMINING FLAT WIDTH</u>

FW X _____ = _____ ÷ _____ = _____ = _____
     Amount of fullness   flat width   WOM   round up to next whole number   number of widths needed

B) <u>DETERMINING FINISHED LENGTH</u>

FL + _____ + _____ = _____ ÷ _____ = _____ ⇒ ⇒ ⇒ ⇒ ⇒ ⇒
    Amount of header   amount of hem   cut length w/o RPT   size of repeat   number of repeats   round up to next whole number

= _____ X _____ = _____
    number of repeats required   size of repeats   total cut length

C) <u>DETERMINING YARDAGE</u>

Multiply A X B to obtain fabric needed _____ X _____ ÷ by 36 = _____ yards
    A) # of widths   B) total

GROMMET DRAPERY PANELS (CONTINUED)

To Make

- Start with the hems. Double fold drapery hems 4", press flat and blind stitch. If you don't own a blind hemmer, use the blind stitch on your sewing machine with the recommended foot, or hem by hand. Set aside and hem lining.

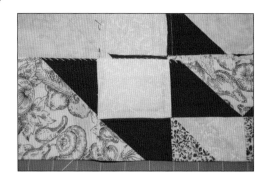

- To hem lining, fold 2" double fold hems, and press flat. Stitch using the Edge Joining Foot or Stitch in the Ditch Foot, with your needle moved to the left just enough to catch the edge of the fold.

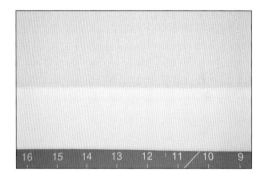

- With wrong sides together, line up the top edges of each hem. (This will make the lining 2" shorter.) Line up seams, and pin together to prevent shifting. Trim selvage off the lining.

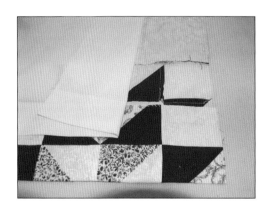

- Press edge over to make a double fold 1 1/4" side hem. Pin into place, but do not sew.

- Measuring from the bottom, mark a pressing line for the top edge of your drapery. If you are using the entire piece, fold over 1" along the top edge, to the backside. Unfold the top corners, so that the top edge is under the side hems. The side hems will be the entire length of the drapery.

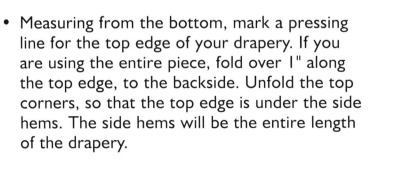

GROMMET DRAPERY PANELS (CONTINUED)

To Make (CONTINUED)

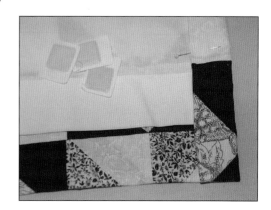

- It's time to sew the side hems. (Yes, sew the sides before the top!) Before your side hems, you'll need to insert your drapery weights. Just unfold the side hem one turn, and place a square drapery weight inside the hem. Pin the side hem in place, and blind hem the side hems, sewing the entire length of the drapery.

Finishing your Drapery

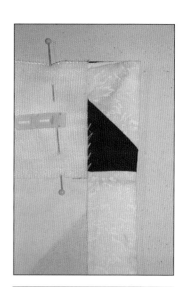

- Using the grommet tape, pin the tape onto the wrong side of the drapery. You will want to use an even number of grommets, so position your tape accordingly.

- You can either sew the tape in place or use Permanent Double Stick Tape to secure grommet tape.

Note: If you choose to sew on the tape, it's recommended that you use a polyester invisible thread in the bobbin, so that the stitching lines will be less visible.

- After securing the grommet tape on your drapery, cut away the fabric inside the grommets.

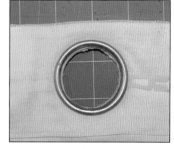

- On the front side, add the ring face to each of the "holes".

- To keep your drapery from pulling flat across the window, secure back tabs as shown. This will keep your folds even across the top of the window.

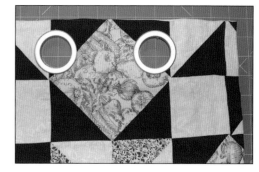

- Your grommet draperies are now ready to hang. Dress draperies with Wrinkle Release Dressing Spray.

A special thank you to Joann Trombley for this lovely quilt top used to make this project.

THE PATCHWORK CHAIR PAD

The quilt top chosen for this project was from my stash. Since it was hand pieced, it wasn't exactly square, but because it was hand pieced, I didn't have the heart to dispose of it. The fun of making something like this chair pad is that they can all be different! My log home is casual so this "Scrappy" look works!

Supplies for each Chair Pad
- 2-20" squares of pieced fabric, plus extra accent fabric for welt cord and ties
- Or if using yardage, about $3/4$ - 1 yard of fabric
- Template paper: This can be brown kraft paper, leftover wallpaper, or newspaper (I used wallpaper)
- Fantastic Fusible Fabric Backing
- Lining: I use drapery lining, but you could also use muslin
- 1" foam
- 1 $1/2$ yard 27" wide upholstery polyester batting
- Zipper Tape by the yard with slide
- About 1 $1/4$ yard of Welt Cord
- Foam Adhesive Spray
- Zipper Foot or Welting Foot
- Stiletto

Note: *These directions are using standard home dec sewing techniques and allowances. A $1/2$" seam allowance is being used throughout this project.*

To Make
- Begin by making a paper template pattern. Place paper on chair seat. Secure with masking or painter's tape to prevent slipping.

- Using a pencil with slightly rounded lead (a too sharp lead will break on you), trace around the edge of the chair. Cut template out leaving about $1/4$" edge outside the pencil mark.

THE PATCHWORK CHAIR PAD (CONTINUED)

To Make (CONTINUED)

- Fold the template in half lengthwise, and trim on the pencil line, giving you a symmetrical shape. (Now, I know what you're thinking, "What if my chair seat is slightly unsymmetrical?" And you're right, it sure might be a bit off, but if the cushion is even on both sides, then you can make it reversible, giving you twice the wear!) To make sure your cushion will be symmetrical fold in half and even out the cutting line. Mark on the paper template where you'll want the ties.

Prep your Fabric

Begin by laying your quilt top out to assess whether you have enough for the project you're making. If you indeed determine that there's not enough fabric some options might be:

- Add more blocks of the same fabric, or similar fabrics to extend to size needed.
- Add a border of a matching or coordinating fabric to extend to size needed.
- Use another quilt top. In the case of this project, I believe it's perfectly acceptable for the chair pads not to match exactly.
- Line the back side of the chair pad patchwork with Fantastic Fusible Fabric Backing.
- Press your top out, using the highest steam setting on your iron. (Press, don't iron!) This will help flatten out the seams, set them and give you a flatter surface to work with. Depending on the stitch quality of your pieced fabric, you may want to stabilize it. Use fusible interfacing to do this. I usually iron interfacing onto the back of the pieced fabric to secure the seams. Cut a lining to match. If you want the thickness of a quilt, add a layer of quilt batting in between the lining and face fabric.

Cutting

- Lay your template on your fabric allowing 1" allowance all the way around. This will give you the 1/2" seam allowance as well as an additional 1/2" to compensate for the thickness of the cushion.

- Cut ties from remaining fabric or from accent fabric after all cushion tops and bottoms are cut.
  Ties are cut: 2" wide by the full width of material, or 2" wide X 42" long. Cut two for each cushion.

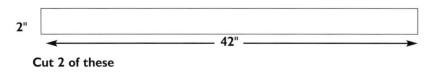

2"

◄——————— 42" ———————►

Cut 2 of these

THE PATCHWORK CHAIR PAD (CONTINUED)

Cutting (CONTINUED)

- Make 2" bias from remaining fabric to cover welt cord. The amount of bias you need will vary with the size of your chair seat. To determine how much welt cord you will need, measure the perimeter of the chair seat using a fabric tape measure.

See Basic Instructions, page 17 to make and apply welt cord.

Sewing your Chair Pad

- If your chair pad has rounded corners like mine, clip as shown to transition the cord at corners, rather than turning a sharp corner as shown in the Basic Instructions, page 17.

- To go around curved corners, like the one shown, clip the cord lip about every 1/2" to ease around the curve.

- Use the Bottom Edge Zipper Insertion on page 20 after the cord is sewn on and spliced. Leave the zipper slide in the center with both ends closed.

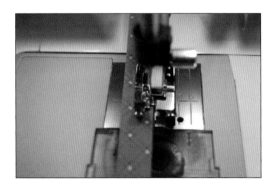

The Ties

- Make your ties by folding in cut edges, and pressing (like double fold bias). Stitch along folded edges and satin stitch across the ends.

Helpful Hint: Using the Edge Stitching Foot (with a center guide), move your needle just a bit to the left of center to topstitch the edge.

- Fold each tie in two at the center, and sew where you've marked for the ties. Backstitch to reinforce.

THE PATCHWORK CHAIR PAD (CONTINUED)

The Ties (CONTINUED)

- Place cushion top and bottom right sides together with the backside of the corded edge up, stitch all the way around the cushion using the cord stitch line as your guide. Sew across zipper ends, and reinforce the ties by back stitching them.

The Cushion Insert

- For best results use new 1" foam, and cover each side with upholstery grade batting. This batting is bonded or glazed, thick and stiff. (Not at all the same as quilt batting!)

- Cut the foam the exact size of your chair seat template.

- Cut the batting also the same size as the template.

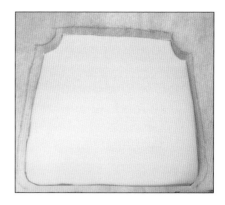

- Spray your foam with a spray adhesive designed for foam. After the foam is covered on both sides, insert into the cushion cover.

- Run your hand across inside, across both top and bottom side to smooth out.

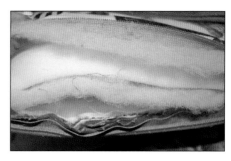

- Zip closed, and admire your new chair pad. If necessary, run a shot of steam over the cushion to smooth out. Sit comfy!

FOOTSTOOL SLIPCOVER

A while back, I was asked to be a guest on the PBS TV show called "It's Sew Easy". At the time, I had just started this book, so I decided to show one of the projects. The project I decide on was the headboard, but since I had limited time, I made a smaller crib size scaled down version. This footstool project came from the leftovers of the TV show and the stool was a yard sale find!

Supplies

- Foot stool to be slipcovered (You can also use a 5 gallon bucket or milk crate!)
- Quilt (or partial quilt) top
- Fabric to make welt cord (see Continuous Bias in Basic Instructions to calculate yardage)
- Welt Cord to wrap around foot stool twice
- Drapery lining (or plain white cotton fabric) to make pattern and line cover
- Flannel interlining
- Hook & Loop Tape
- Fantastic Fusible Fabric Backing
- Bonded Upholstery Batting

To Make

- Start out with a footstool with good "bones".

- Using drapery lining, make your pattern, by pinning onto stool and trimming. Allow for a 1/2" seam allowance.

- Cut the boxing out of lining; allow for 1/2" seam allowance.

FOOTSTOOL SLIPCOVER (CONTINUED)

To Make (CONTINUED)

- Position your quilt top to center a desired motif.

- Using your lining pattern, cut out your top.

- Back the foot stool top with Fantastic Fusible Fabric Backing to prevent frays or seams from coming apart.

- We were able to get enough of these Churn Dash Blocks from the quilt top to make it all the way around the foot stool. Use the rise lining piece to cut these to size. Back with the Fantastic Fusible Fabric Backing.

- Sandwich the fused top with a layer of interlining and the lining pattern. Set aside.

- For information to make enough 2 $1/4$" welt cord to cover the top edge, use Basic Instructions for Continuous Bias, page 10.

FOOTSTOOL SLIPCOVER (CONTINUED)

To Make (CONTINUED)

- See Basic Instructions for Welt Cord, page 17 for making and sewing welt cord onto top.

- Sew boxing onto the top.

- To make the welt cord for the bottom, cut bias 2 1/4" wide, and sew with one side wider than the other.

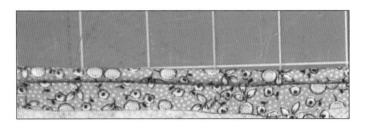

- Sew onto the bottom edge, with the wide side as the right side, facing the cover.

- Splice, according to the Basic Instructions for Welt Cord, page 17.

- When you fold it down, the wider side will be a lip to attach the loop side of the Hook & Loop Tape.

- Staple the hook side of the Hook & Loop Tape on the bottom of the footstool.

- Sew the loop side of the Hook & Loop Tape on the footstool cover. Snip the welt cord lip at the corners where the legs are and tuck excess under.

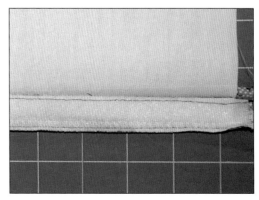

- Serge bottom edges and seams.

- If needed make a "slip" out of batting to give a fuller look.

Thank you to JoAnn Trombley for this quilt top.

3-D Star Pillow

3-D STAR PILLOW

This star pillow is a design that won the 2009 pillow competition at the IWCE in Atlanta, GA. The gentleman (Ray) who won whipped it up, giving me the basic idea of how it was made. The idea was his, but the directions are mine, so if it isn't exactly like yours, Ray, forgive me!

Supplies

- For the pillow shown: 15 - 7" to 10" quilt blocks or 2/3 yard of 45 to 54" wide fabric
- 8"-10" Zipper Tape one Zipper Slide
- Pam's Perfect Puff-n-Stuff®
- Two large buttons (I used matching covered buttons)

To Make

- You will need to cut 15 squares of fabric. These blocks measured 7", which gives me a 16" pillow.

- If you want your pillow smaller or larger, cut your squares accordingly. Your pillow will be about twice the size as your cut squares.

- Sew the 5 sections as shown, stitching with 1/2" seam allowances when using regular fabric; 1/4" seam allowances when using quilt blocks. Stop sewing 1/4" or 1/2" from the ends of each seam, depending on which seam allowance you're using, and back stitch at the end of each seam.

- After sewing the first 5 sections together as shown, sew another 5 sections together, making the pillow front and back.

- Trim seam allowances at center to eliminate excess bulk. Press all seams open and flat.

- The 5 remaining squares will be the pillow sides. Sew each square onto pillow front, sewing two perpendicular sides. You will need to insert your zipper on one of these sides.

3-D STAR PILLOW (CONTINUED)

Zipper Insertion

- Separate zipper tape and sew one side of zipper tape to pillow front and sew the other side to a side square.

- Using the larger end of the slide (the end with 2 holes) install slide as shown. Pull slide all the way off and reinstall. This will give you a sealed zipper at both ends, so your project will go together easier.

- Sew across the ends of the zipper as you assemble the pillow will keep the ends secure.

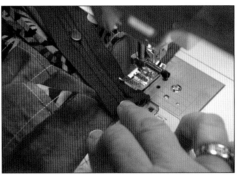

- Sew all 5 side squares onto one side of the pillow, sewing just two sides of each side square. Press all seams open and flat.

- You will have two sides of each side square unsewn, ready for the other side of your pillow. Sew other side onto remaining two sides of each side squares.

Note: *You may find it easier to sew the outside squares if you keep them to the bottom with the seamed pillow on top.*

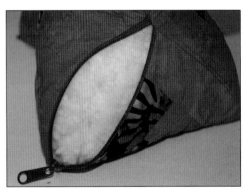

- Clip excess fabric in corners, press seams open and flat.

- Turn right sides out through the zipper opening. Stuff with a good quality virgin polyester fiber fill. We use "Pam's Perfect Puff-n-Stuff®". Close zipper, and steam pillow if necessary.

- To cinch in the center, use heavy buttonhole/ carpet thread, with a long upholstery needle. Knot thread, and loop through one button. With a long needle, pull through pillow center, catch the other button, and pull taut. You will want to run your thread through about 4-5 times, and knot to secure.

ORPHAN BLOCK PILLOW ONE

This was a block from a techniques class I took on fabric folding. The block measured 8" before the pillow project was started. This pillow finishes at 16" square. (To make this quilt block, refer to the book: Fantastic Fabric Folding by Rebecca Wat.)

Supplies

- 2 fabrics that coordinate with your block
- Fat quarter for pillow back
- 3/8 yard fabric for pleated trim
- 3/8 yard fabric for shirred welting
- 1 1/2 yards of two coordinating pieces of Ric Rac
- 1/4" wide Steam-a-Seam 2
- 3/8" Permanent Double Stick Tape
- 17" Zipper Tape with one slide
- 17" Square of Fusi-boo Quilt Batting or regular quilt batting and temporary spray adhesive
- Ultimate Pillow Template
- Pillow form or Pam's Perfect Puff & Stuff®

To Make

- Start off with an 8" quilt block similar to this.
- Cut two squares, 6" and cut diagonally to make 4 triangles.
- Sew two triangles to opposite sides of block.
- Sew remaining two triangles to make a square.

Mitered Border

- Cut four strips that measure 3 1/2" by 20".
- Centering each strip, sew onto block, stopping 1/4" from the corner.

ORPHAN BLOCK PILLOW ONE (CONTINUED)

Mitered Border (CONTINUED)

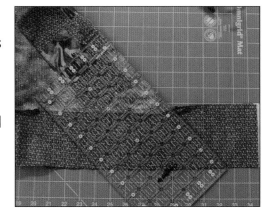

- Fold pillow diagonally at each corner, lining edges up together and matching seams together.

- Using a straight edge ruler lined up on the diagonal fold, draw a stitching line for the mitered border.

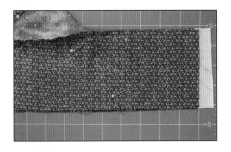

- Pin along line and stitch on line.

- Trim to a $1/4$" seam allowance.

- Press mitered seam open.

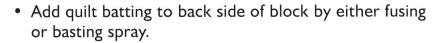

- Add quilt batting to back side of block by either fusing or basting spray.

- Outline quilt either by machine, by hand, or by Sashiko Machine as shown here.

- Taper pillow corners using the Ultimate Pillow Template. (see page16)

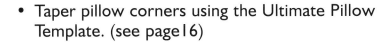

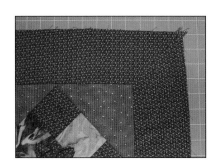

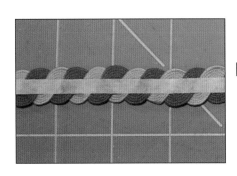

Ric Rac Trim

- To make Ric Rac trim, please refer to Basic Instructions, page 24.

ORPHAN BLOCK PILLOW ONE (CONTINUED)

To Make (CONTINUED)

- Apply ¹/4" Steam a Seam to one side of the Ric Rac trim.

- Pin the Ric Rac into place and press, securing with the Steam-a-Seam. Line up for the splice.

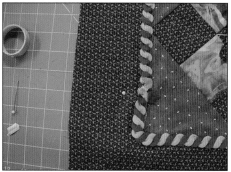

- Place a small amount of permanent double stick tape across the Ric Rac where the other color will overlap. Trim across where the tape is.

- Overlap with the other color, tucking raw ends under opposite color so that each color cover the splice of the other.

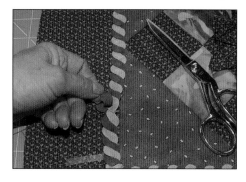

- Using either a twin needle to coverstitch (shown) on your serger, sew Ric Rac trim to secure.

- To add Shirred Welt trim, please refer to Basic Instructions, page 15. Splice as you would for standard welt cord.

- If adding optional Box Pleat Trim, apply to the back side of the pillow. (See Basic Instructions, page 8)

- Using the bottom edge zipper insertion method on page 20, put one side of the zipper into each side of the pillow. Marry the zipper together and sew remaining sides to complete pillow.

ORPHAN BLOCK PILLOW TWO

This was a Grandmother's Flower Garden block made from a Quiltsmart® block. Since there was only one block, a pillow was the perfect way to finish it. This pillow is complimented with machine "hand quilting", box pleated trim and Ric Rac. Finished size: 16"

Supplies

- Fat quarter for pillow front
- Fat quarter for pillow back
- 3/8 yard fabric for pleated trim
- 2 yards of coordinating Ric Rac
- 17" Zipper Tape with one slide
- 17" Square of Fusi-boo quilt batting, or regular quilt batting and temporary spray adhesive
- Pillow form or Pam's Perfect Puff & Stuff®
- Appliqué or Open Toe Foot
- Ultimate Pillow Template
- Box Pleat Tape

To Make

- Trim pillow front fabric to a 17" square, using the Ultimate Pillow Template and fuse quilt batting to the back.

- Using an appliqué or satin stitch, sew block onto background fabric.

- Echo quilt around your block either by machine, by hand or by Sashiko Machine.

ORPHAN BLOCK PILLOW TWO (CONTINUED)

To Make (CONTINUED)

- Using the Ultimate Pillow Template, trim the dog ears before adding any edge trim.

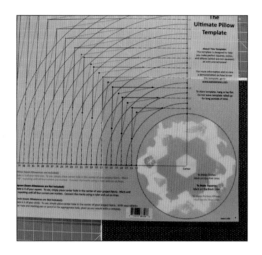 

- Sew Ric Rac by machine or Fashiko 1" from raw edge.

- Make 1" Box Pleat Trim, (Refer to Basic Instructions, page 8), and sew onto the front side of the pillow.

- Insert zipper into the bottom edge, using the Bottom Edge Insertion method found on page 20.

- Sew three remaining sides. Serge seams and turn right sides out. Stuff with Pam's Perfect Puff & Stuff®.

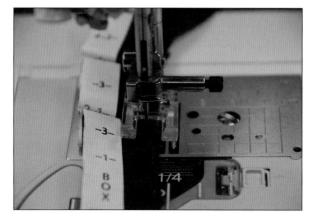

ORPHAN BLOCK MINI BAGS

Even a basic Nine Patch Block can be made into something useful and fun. Here are two projects made from the same block. The Zipper Tape available on www.pamdamour.com has a reversible coil, so you can make a bag using only one half of the zipper!

The Square Bag

Supplies

- 9" to 10" block
- Backing and Fusi-boo batting to match block
- 20" of zipper tape and one slide
  (If making both bags, you'll need 20" of zipper tape and two slides)
- Machine quilting thread

To Make

- With your iron, press the three layers (quilt block, batting and backing together, according to the instructions on the batting package.
- Machine or hand quilt as desired.

Note: *This block was quilted using Babylock's Sashiko Machine.*

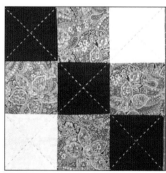

- Fold block in half and sew ends with a ¹/2" seam allowance.

- Separate the zipper, and use one side for this bag.

ORPHAN BLOCK MINI BAGS (CONTINUED)

To Make (CONTINUED)

- Find the center on one edge and start zipper, leaving 1/2" of zipper end extending. Sew with teeth facing down.

- Sew all the way around, till your zipper end meets the beginning end.

- Snip the seam allowance of the bag, between where the two zipper ends meet.

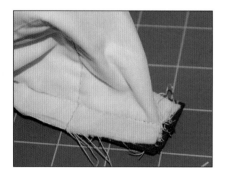

- Install the slide and sew across the zipper ends as shown.

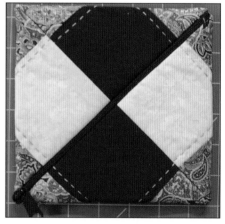

- Turn right side out and press flat.

The Rectangular Bag

Supplies
- 9" to 10" block
- Backing and Fusi-boo batting to match block
- 20" of zipper tape and one slide
  (If making both bags, you'll need 20" of zipper tape and two slides.)
- Machine quilting thread

ORPHAN BLOCK MINI BAGS (CONTINUED)

To Make (CONTINUED)

Rectangular Bag

- With your iron, press the three layers (quilt block, batting and backing together), according to the instructions on the batting package.

- Machine or hand quilt as desired.

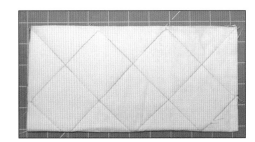

Note: This block was quilted using Babylock's Sashiko Machine.

- Fold block in half and sew one end only with a ¹/₂" seam allowance.

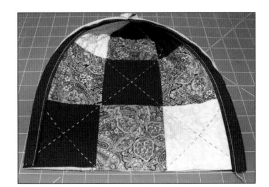

- Separate the zipper, and use one side for this bag.

- Sew one side of the zipper along the top edge with the teeth facing down. Open seam as you sew over the zipper.

- Install zipper slide and sew remaining side.

- Turn right sides out and press flat.

Quilt Block Bag

QUILT BLOCK BAG

This cute bag was made from two blocks leftover from a quilt made from fabrics purchased in Australia.

Supplies

- Two quilt blocks 7" to 8" square
- Lining and batting to match blocks
- 1 1/4 yard of 3" wide bias fabric for pleated trim
- 12" Zipper tape with one slide
- Box pleat tape
- Permanent Double Stick Tape
- 1 1/4 yards of two coordinating pieces of Ric Rac for optional strap

To Make

- Trim lining and batting to match blocks. Layer block with batting only.

- Make box pleat trim and sew onto top edge. Keep pleated trim 5/8" from each edge. Fold raw edges inside toward each other and secure with Permanent Double Stick Tape.

- Pin into place and sew at 1/2" seam allowance.

- If making the optional strap, insert each end near bag corners before sewing on ruffle.

Note: Optional strap is made like the Ric Rac trim on page 24 and secured with a Zig Zag stitch down the center.

- Pin one side of zipper as shown. Snip seam allowances on zipper tape so that it will turn the corners.

Quilt Block Bag

QUILT BLOCK BAG (CONTINUED)

To Make (CONTINUED)

- Sew zipper along both tops edges of bag, turning corner and sewing down 2" on each side.

- Sew lining where zipper is, stopping $1/2$" from each end of the zipper.

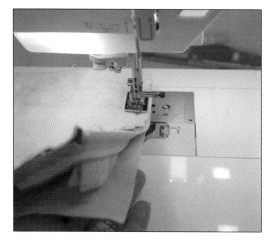

- Turn right sides out and marry zipper together. Pull slide all the way off and put back on a second time leaving both zipper ends sealed shut.

- Snip seam allowances at the end of the stitching along the sides. With all the raw edges together, sew sides and bottom.

- Finish by serging raw edges together.

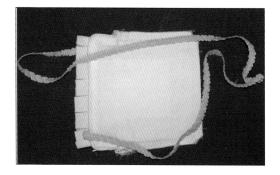

- Turn right side out and press flat.

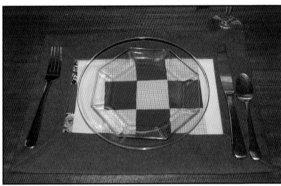

Chair

This seat cover and chair back cover are made from a quilt top.
The purple bias trim and embroidery complete the ensemble.

Table Runner

A leftover strip of blocks sewn on point make a perfect table runner.

Placemat

This denim mitered frame holds leftover quilt blocks to make a scrappy placemat.

Pillow

An unfinished fused appliqué block finishes into a lovely pillow complimented
with a plaid back and piping.

Acknowledgements

*T*hank you to the following companies who provided us with support through their products and machines. We hope you will thank these companies by supporting them.

BERNINA

made to create

JANOME

Robison-Anton RA

YKK

Glossary of Sewing and Quilting Terms

Note: *You'll find terms here not in this book, but I included them so you could use this as a reference guide for all your sewing projects.*

Basting
   Temporary stitches used to create gathers, or to temporarily sew something together.
   The stitches are usually 3.5-4.5mm in length and are taken out when the project is completed.

Basting in the Hoop
   This is also known as fixing in the hoop. It is done in the embroidery function/mode of
   your sewing machine and is a series, usually a square or rectangle, of basting stitches.
   These stitches outline your design area as well as tack layers of fabric or stabilizers together.

Bias
   If something is cut on the true bias, it is cut at 45 degrees to the selvage or at a diagonal line
   across the fabric.

Bias Band
   A strip of fabric cut on the bias, and applied onto another fabric.

Buckram
   A stiff starched fabric inserted in sewing projects to add stability and body. In draperies, it's
   usually in 4" strips and used in the top or header of the panel.

Cross Grain
   When fabric is cut at right angles to the grain line, across the grain, selvage to selvage.

Deck or Decking
   The piece of fabric,(usually lining) that is in between the mattress and box spring on a bed skirt.
   It can also be the fabric under the cushion on an upholstered or slipcovered piece of furniture.

Fabric Grain
   The direction of the fabric, up and down the length or perpendicular to the selvedge. They
   are called the lengthwise grain, crosswise grain and the bias.

Finished Width or FW
   The finished width of a window treatment after it's pleated, or gathered and mounted on a
   board or rod.

Hook & Loop Tape
   Known by its brand name, Velcro®.

Hemostats
   A locking pair of pliers similar to needle nose. They're usually used as a clamp in the medical field.

Interlining
   A fabric between the outside fabric and the lining usually used to add texture/structure to a
   project. Interlining is usually a white or natural flannel.

Lining
   This is a lightweight fabric that lines a project. It prevents lighter weight fabrics from being
   too sheer as well. Linings can complement the outside fabric or contrast for an exciting inside
   personality to your project.

Long Point
   The longest point of a window treatment. Often it's the tail section, but not always!

Mounting
   The process of securing your design to a wood pole or wood board, before installing.

Miter
   The technique when binding a project that results in 45-degree corners on a right angle.

Nap
   A one-way direction of texture on a fabric such as velvet or corduroy. When using fabric with a
   nap all pieces must be cut with the nap in the same direction.

Glossary of Sewing and Quilting Terms

Placket

An extra piece of fabric, usually about 2" and added to the bottom of the pillow below the zipper.

Pillowcasing

In decorating, the term pillowcasing refers to the techniques of sewing the bottom and sides of a project in one continuous row of stitching, like a pillowcase!! Generally, after pillowcasing a project, the next step is to turn right sides out, and press flat.

Piping

A decorated or covered cording inserted into the seam of a project for decoration; also known as welting.

Pivot

Turning a corner or angle while your needle is in the fabric and the presser foot is raised to prevent fabric from shifting.

Railroading

The method of using fabric horizontally, rather than vertically, which is the traditional method in home dec sewing.

Raw Edge

The cut edge of a project. It may fray or ravel if left in this state.

Returns

The projection of a window treatment, or where the design "returns" back to the wall. It's also the width of the board the design is mounted on.

Right Side (RS)

Right side, usually in reference to the right side of fabric, which is the side of the fabric with the print or finish.

Right Side Together (RST)

Right sides together. A term meaning that two pieces of fabric should have the right sides facing each other before you sew.

Seam Allowance

The fabric between the cut edge of the project and the seam line. This measurement varies based on the type of project you are doing. This book was written with the standard 1/2" seam allowances, unless otherwise specified.

Seam Ripper

A sewer's best friend! Used to remove basting stitches as well as "accidents".

Selvage

The woven edge of the fabric. One of the selvages usually has printing on it.

Short Point

The shortest point on the window treatment. It's important to know the short point, so the valance can be installed at the best height above the window.

Straight Grain

The direction of the threads traveling parallel to the selvage.

Tail

Refers to the long point section of a window treatment, as it frames the window.

Top Stitching

A decorative stitch like edge stitching, but further from the edge of the garment. They can come in multiple rows and look very nice.

Wrong Side (WS)

Wrong side, usually in reference to the wrong side of fabric. This side of the fabric is bland and usually has a muted version of the print side of the fabric.

Wrong Sides Together (WST)

Wrong sides together, the two fabrics that are to be sewn together have the wrong sides of the fabric touching.

Product List

The follow are available at www.pamdamour.com

- Beaded Weight Chain
- Box Pleat Tape
- Brass Stiletto
- Continuous Prairie Point Ruler
- Drapery Weights
- Fantastic Fusible Fabric Backing®
- FriXion Pen
- Grommet Tape
- Headboard Mounting Cleat
- Home Dec Ruler
- Home Decorators Proportional Scale
- Jumbo Welt
- Katie Lane Scallop Radial Rule
- Knife Pleat Tape
- Micro Welt
- Pam's Perfect Puff-n-Stuff®
- Permanent Double Stick Tape
- Pocket Scissors
- Roman Shade Cord Lock
- Roman Shade Cord Tassels
- Roman Shade Lift Cord Adjusters
- Roman Shade Ribs
- Roman Shade Screw Eyes
- Roman Shade Sew-on Rings
- Ultimate Pillow Template
- Welt Cord
- Workroom Push Pins
- Wrinkle Release
- Zipper Tape

**PAM DAMOUR
THE DECORATING DIVA**
495 Point Au Fer Road
Champlain, New York 12919
pam@pamdamour.com
www.pamdamour.com

Index

Index

Index

Inspirations

Linda's Bed

This collection was made by my good friend, Linda Visnaw who wanted to show how a quilt can be incorporated with my "Poodle Skirt" template pattern #6 from my *Cheaper by the Dozen* book. Using this valance pattern can create a lovely skirt, that when added to a quilt makes a beautiful bedspread. The matching pillow sham has double welting.